EDGE
BOOKS

Top Crossbreed Dogs

COCKAPOO

Cocker Spaniels Meet Poodles!

by Paula M. Wilson

Raintree is an imprint of Capstone Global Library Limited, a company incorporated in England and Wales having its registered office at 264 Banbury Road, Oxford, OX2 7DY – Registered company number: 6695582

www.raintree.co.uk
myorders@raintree.co.uk

Editor: Maddie Spalding
Designer and Production Specialist: Laura Polzin
Printed and bound in India

ISBN: 978 1 4747 6854 2
10 9 8 7 6 5 4 3 2 1
23 22 21 20 19

British Library Cataloguing in Publication Data
A full catalogue record for this book is available from the British Library.

Acknowledgements
AP Images: Maura Lynch, 22–23; iStockphoto: DACowley, 9, 24–25, fantail, 6–7, martinasphotography, 16–17; Newscom: John Short, 18–19, 28–29; Shutterstock Images: Anna K Majer, 12–13, Annmarie Young, 20–21, Caleb Foster, 4–5, Daisy Daisy, 26–27, David Charles Cottam, cover, SikorskiFotografie, 14–15, Vera Zinkova, 10–11.
Design elements: bittbox.

Every effort has been made to contact copyright holders of material reproduced in this book. Any omissions will be rectified in subsequent printings if notice is given to the publisher.

All the internet addresses (URLs) given in this book were valid at the time of going to press. However, due to the dynamic nature of the internet, some addresses may have changed, or sites may have changed or ceased to exist since publication. While the author and publisher regret any inconvenience this may cause readers, no responsibility for any such changes can be accepted by either the author or the publisher.

CONTENTS

CHAPTER ONE

MEET THE COCKAPOO

Do you like small dogs that look like teddy bears? Then the Cockapoo may be the right dog for your family! Cockapoos are small dogs with thick, wavy fur. They have big, round eyes and button noses. They are friendly and fun-loving dogs. Although they love to run and play, Cockapoos also like to snuggle with people and take a nap.

Cockapoos are a type of crossbreed dog. A crossbreed dog is a cross between two **breeds**. The breeds are usually chosen for certain traits, or qualities. A Cockapoo is a cross between a Cocker Spaniel and a Poodle. Cocker Spaniels and Poodles are **purebred** dogs. Cockapoos get their traits from both of these breeds.

breed a type of dog that has specific traits

purebred a dog that is the same breed as its parents

Cockapoos have soft, fluffy fur.

A LOYAL COMPANION

Cockapoos fit well into a busy family's lifestyle. These dogs like to be around people. They quickly become entertaining and loving members of the family. Cockapoos make wonderful family pets no matter where you live. Do you live in a flat or a small home? No problem. Most Cockapoos are small and do not need much space. Or maybe you live in a house with a big garden. Cockapoos will love to run and play in the grass.

Fact!

Cockapoos are a big hit on Instagram. One Cockapoo called Oliver has over 5,000 followers!

Cockapoos like to run and play.

CHAPTER TWO

COCKAPOO HISTORY

Breeders have been crossing dog breeds for many years. They mixed different breeds together to produce dogs with certain traits, such as hunting and herding skills. Today, crossbreed dogs are usually bred to become pets, not working dogs. People seek out Cockapoos because they want a friendly and snuggly companion.

THE FIRST CROSSBREED

Some people say that Cockapoos started the crossbreed dog craze. Cockapoos were first bred in the United States in the 1950s. No one knows why the first Cockapoos were bred. Many people believe they were bred by accident.

 breeder someone who brings dogs together so they can breed, or reproduce

Cockapoos have been popular pets for more than 50 years.

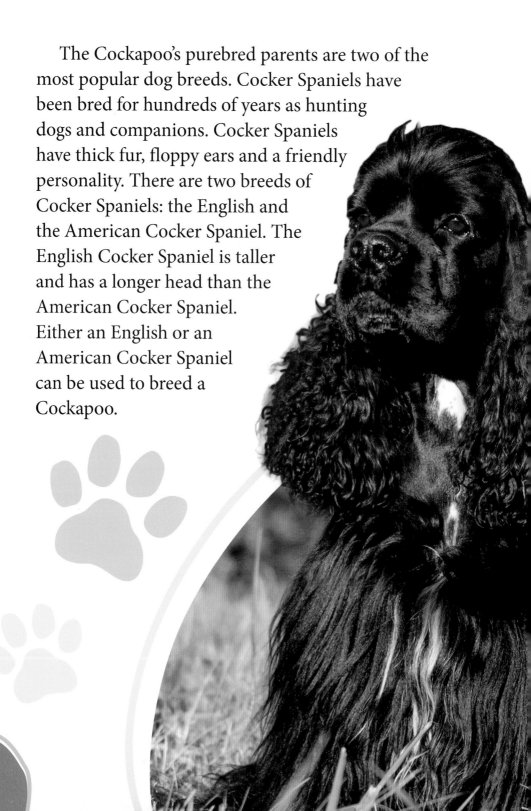

The Cockapoo's purebred parents are two of the most popular dog breeds. Cocker Spaniels have been bred for hundreds of years as hunting dogs and companions. Cocker Spaniels have thick fur, floppy ears and a friendly personality. There are two breeds of Cocker Spaniels: the English and the American Cocker Spaniel. The English Cocker Spaniel is taller and has a longer head than the American Cocker Spaniel. Either an English or an American Cocker Spaniel can be used to breed a Cockapoo.

Cocker Spaniels have long, wavy fur.

Poodles have long been known as show dogs. But for centuries people have also bred Poodles as hunting dogs. They leap into the water to fetch birds that their owners hunt. Poodles are playful and highly intelligent. They also shed less than other types of dogs. This is good news for people who are allergic to dogs. Dogs that shed less produce less dander. Dander is flakes of dry skin that make people with dog allergies sneeze and get watery, itchy eyes. Cockapoos can **inherit** traits from both their Poodle and Cocker Spaniel parents. They have many of the traits people find desirable in Poodles and Cocker Spaniels.

POPULAR POOCHES

The Cockapoo is one of the most popular crossbreed dogs. In the years since they were first bred, Cockapoos have gained a large following. Cockapoos are especially popular in the UK and the United States. But their popularity extends worldwide.

 inherit receive a trait from a parent or ancestor

Fact!
Many celebrities
own Cockapoos.
Actresses Ashley Judd and
Jennifer Aniston own Cockapoos.
Singer Lady Gaga
also owns a Cockapoo.

*Poodles have thick,
curly fur.*

CHAPTER THREE

ALL ABOUT THE COCKAPOO

Cockapoos are not all the same size. Some Cockapoos are bigger or taller than others. The size of a Cockapoo depends on the size of its Poodle parent. The smallest Cockapoos are called toy Cockapoos. They grow to about 25 centimetres (10 inches) tall. They weigh about 5 kilograms (12 pounds). Mini Cockapoos are usually 28 to 36 cm (11 to 14 inches) tall. They usually weigh 5 to 9 kg (12 to 20 pounds). Standard Cockapoos are about 38 cm (15 inches) tall. They typically weigh about 9 kg (20 pounds).

Fact!

Some Cockapoos sleep flat on their backs with their legs up in the air and their heads thrown back. Cockapoo owners often call this the "poo pose"! Many people enjoy taking photos of their Cockapoos in these funny positions.

Even the largest Cockapoos are smaller than many other dogs.

Cockapoos can have many colour combinations. Common colours include black, brown, white, apricot, cream and red. Some Cockapoos are a single colour. Other Cockapoos have coats with two or even three colours. A Cockapoo's coat colour may change as the dog gets older. Some Cockapoos have thick and silky coats that are slightly wavy, similar to the Cocker Spaniel's coat. Some Cockapoos have very curly coats, similar to the Poodle's coat.

Fact!

A Cockapoo may inherit a certain Poodle **gene** that controls its coat colour. Its coat colour may fade to a lighter shade as it ages.

PLEASING PERSONALITIES

Along with physical traits, Cockapoos can also inherit personality traits from Cocker Spaniels and Poodles. Cockapoos are often calm and friendly like the Cocker Spaniel. They are also clever and do not shed much. They get these traits from the Poodle. Because of their easygoing manner, Cockapoos often get on well with small children and other pets. They make fun companions because they are often loyal and eager to please.

 gene part of a cell in an animal's body that determines the animal's appearance and other traits

Therapy Cockapoos

Some Cockapoos work as therapy dogs. Therapy dogs help comfort people who are sick or have disabilities. Cockapoos tend to have a gentle and loving personality, so they make great therapy dogs. In the UK, a Cockapoo called Bilbo Baggins won the Crufts Therapy Dog of the Year award in 2016. Bilbo is a cuddly black Cockapoo that visits a school for children with disabilities. He helps children to feel calm.

Some Cockapoos' coats have a combination of colours.

CHAPTER FOUR

CARING FOR YOUR COCKAPOO

All dogs need proper care to stay healthy. Before deciding to get a Cockapoo, your family should think about what a Cockapoo will need. When you take good care of your Cockapoo, you help it stay happy and healthy.

If your family is ready for a Cockapoo, finding a licensed breeder is a good place to start. Cockapoo breeders can help you decide which dog is right for you. They can also show you how to care for a Cockapoo. You should ask the breeder whether the Cockapoo has been to a vet and received the injections it needs. You should also ask about the dog's family history. Then you can see whether certain health conditions run in the dog's family. This will help prepare you and your family for health conditions that the Cockapoo may have.

Cockapoos need daily exercise and playtime.

Fact!

Cockapoo clubs such as the British Cockapoo Society educate people about the Cockapoo. These clubs share information about how to find responsible Cockapoo breeders.

Another option is to find a local animal sanctuary or rescue centre. They may have Cockapoos that your family can adopt. Ask people at the sanctuary or centre if they have information about the Cockapoo's background. The more information you have about your new pet, the better prepared you will be to take good care of it.

Your family should also talk to your vet about having your Cockapoo neutered or spayed. Neutering involves removing a part of a male animal's body that helps it make babies.

Cockapoo puppies have different nutritional needs from adult Cockapoos.

Spaying is the same process, but it is done for a female. Dogs that aren't neutered or spayed may give birth to many puppies. It can be hard for one family to care for or find homes for many puppies.

DIET AND REST

When Cockapoos are young they should be fed a dog food made especially for puppies. Puppy food has **nutrients** that help Cockapoo puppies grow. As your Cockapoo gets older, you should give it dog food made for small-breed dogs.

nutrient a substance needed for healthy growth and development

Professional groomers can style and trim your Cockapoo's fur.

You should feed your Cockapoo twice each day. Your dog's first meal should be in the morning. Then you should feed your Cockapoo once in the evening. This keeps you and your dog on a steady schedule.

You should measure out your Cockapoo's food at each meal. This will help your dog remain at a steady and healthy weight. Making sure your Cockapoo does not overeat is important.

Your Cockapoo should also get plenty of rest throughout the day. Dogs sleep for about 12 to 14 hours each day. They nap many times in a day. Make sure your Cockapoo has a comfortable area to sleep, such as a crate or a special spot in your home.

GROOMING AND CARE

All dogs need to be **groomed**. Grooming includes cleaning and combing your dog's coat. A Cockapoo's coat should be combed about once every few days so its fur does not clump or get knotted. Your family should take your Cockapoo to a groomer at least once every eight weeks. Professional groomers know how to properly wash, brush and trim a Cockapoo's coat.

groom care for a dog's coat

Just like your teeth, you should brush your Cockapoo's teeth every day. Keeping your dog's teeth clean prevents **tooth decay** and gum problems. Your Cockapoo's nails should be trimmed once every few months. Your vet can teach you how to trim your dog's nails properly. And don't forget about your pet's eyes and ears! They should be regularly wiped clean to prevent **infections**.

EXERCISE AND SOCIALIZING

Keeping your Cockapoo active is important for your dog's health. Daily walks keep your Cockapoo fit and entertained. Your family should exercise your Cockapoo for about one hour each day. Another way to keep your Cockapoo active is to play with it. Fun games include throwing a ball for it to fetch, running around the garden or hiding something for it to find.

 tooth decay when bacteria destroy the outer surface of a tooth

infection a condition that occurs when germs such as bacteria and viruses get inside an animal's body

If your Cockapoo goes for a swim, you should dry its ears afterwards to prevent an ear infection.

Water dogs

Cockapoos are often good swimmers. Swimming is a great form of exercise. Because Cockapoos don't have very thick hair, they don't get weighed down in the water like some dogs. This helps them swim easily. When swimming in deep water, it can be useful for your Cockapoo to wear a special dog life jacket or vest.

Training can be fun for you and your Cockapoo.

Cockapoos need to exercise their brain as well. Cockapoos are clever and may get bored easily. Some owners teach their Cockapoos to do tricks. They set up obstacle courses for their Cockapoos to master. These tasks can help keep your Cockapoo entertained. Because Cockapoos are clever, training them is often easier than training other dog breeds. Still, training takes patience and lots of repetition. Cockapoos respond well to positive training commands, not punishment. You should be gentle yet firm when training your Cockapoo. Give them rewards for their efforts.

Another important part of caring for your Cockapoo is socializing it. Socializing a dog helps it to be calm around people and other animals. Dogs who are not socialized may become nervous and afraid when faced with new situations. You can socialize your Cockapoo by arranging play times with other dogs. The other dogs should be similar in size and energy level to your Cockapoo.

HEALTH ISSUES

Cockapoos sometimes inherit health problems from their purebred parents. Common health issues include hip and elbow dysplasia. In hip dysplasia, the upper leg bone does not fit snugly into the hip **joint**. Elbow dysplasia usually occurs when a dog's elbow bones do not grow properly. This can lead to swelling and joint pain.

Cockapoos may also have an eye problem called progressive retinal atrophy (PRA). The retina is a part of the eye. It receives images and sends signals to the brain so the brain can identify images. PRA damages the retina over time. A dog with PRA will lose part or all of its vision.

Vets can usually treat these health issues with medicine or surgery. Sometimes a special diet and exercise helps these problems get better. You should take your Cockapoo to the vet at least once a year for a check-up. Your vet will also give your Cockapoo **vaccinations** to help protect it against diseases.

 joint the point where two bones join together in the body

vaccination a shot that contains a substance made up of dead, weakened or living organisms, which protects a person or animal from a disease

ALL-AROUND FUN

Cockapoos are not just cute and cuddly. They are also devoted companions. Having a Cockapoo as a furry member of your family is loads of fun!

Cockapoos are playful and fun companions.

GLOSSARY

breed a type of dog that has specific traits

breeder someone who brings dogs together so they can breed, or reproduce

gene part of a cell in an animal's body that determines the animal's appearance and other traits

groom care for a dog's coat

infection a condition that occurs when germs such as bacteria and viruses get inside an animal's body

inherit receive a trait from a parent or ancestor

joint the point where two bones join together in the body

nutrient a substance needed for healthy growth and development

purebred a dog that is the same breed as its parents

tooth decay when bacteria destroy the outer surface of a tooth

vaccination a shot that contains a substance made up of dead, weakened or living organisms, which protects a person or animal from a disease

FIND OUT MORE

BOOKS

Dogs (Animal Family Albums), Paul Mason (Raintree, 2013)

The Dog Encyclopedia for Kids, Tammy Gagne (Raintree, 2017)

The Truth about Dogs: What Dogs Do When You're Not Looking (Pets Undercover!), Mary Colson (Raintree, 2017)

WEBSITES

The British Cockapoo Society has plenty of information about Cockapoos:
www.britishcockapoosociety.com

The Cockapoo Club of Great Britain also has lots of facts and information about this breed:
www.cockapooclubgb.co.uk

Find out lots of fun Cockapoo facts, including breed characteristics, personality and its history:
dogtime.com/dog-breeds/cockapoo

INDEX